Notes from the Publisher

Welcome to a glimpse into the world of international quilting. At Stitch Publications our wish is for you to be able to explore beyond the boundaries of the country in which you live by experiencing and seeing what other fiber artists are doing.

In many countries, rather than learning from various books, quilters study under a single master, spending years progressing from simple techniques to the extremely difficult. Intricate designs are celebrated and sewing and quilting by hand is honored, and as such, hand quilting is the typical method used to quilt.

This book was written in its original language, Japanese, by a master quilter and artist, Yukari Takahara. We have done our best to make the directions easy to understand if you have some level of quilting experience, while maintaining the appearance and intent of the original author and publisher.

Much of this book is inspirational. By this we mean that there are not necessarily patterns for all the quilts you see in this book; rather it is a book to help you understand the process of designing and putting patterns together for your own story quilts. This is Ms. Takahara's second book on story quilts. Her first book, *Story Quilts - Through the Seasons*, includes many more techniques than this second one.

We hope the beautifully designed handmade items in this book inspire and encourage you to make them for yourself.

- Important Tips Before You Begin -

The following facts might suggest that intermediate or advanced quilters will be more comfortable working on these projects.

- Techniques -

Beyond the "Basic Appliqué Lessons" and "Advanced Designs" sections (starting on p. 80), Ms. Takahara does not go into detailed descriptions of specific quilting, sewing or embroidery methods for each project. She assumes that the creator is familiar with sewing, quilting, and embroidery techniques to some degree and, thus, relies heavily on the creator's ability to figure out the directions that are not specifically written out. It is advisable to understand the basics of appliqué, quilting, and embroidery if you are going to tackle designing your own story quilts.

- Measurements -

There are no measurements given in this book.

- Patterns/Templates -

The patterns that are given on the pages of this book are each used in various quilt vignettes shown. They are examples that can be used for your own quilts and may be used at the size given or shrunk or magnified to the desired size.

Stitch Publications, 2015

Story Quilts 2 - Day by Day

by Yukari Takahara

Story Quilts 2 - Day by Day is the second book by Yukari Takahara. Her first book, *Story Quilts - Through the Seasons*, is the story of her journey as an artist and how she designs and makes her own story quilts. While it is not necessary to your quilting creations, it is a precursor to this one and an excellent companion book as it is full of techniques and approaches to creating your own story quilts.

Whenever I begin any new work of art, I start by sitting down to draw. The first rough sketch is a line drawing - a simple black and white picture that captures the story I want to tell. Before long, I add details that become the prototype for the quilt top.

The most exciting part for me is when I start to pick out different fabrics consisting of all colors and textures for the various designs to build my story quilt. The story seen in fabric is brought to life in a completely different way than when it was merely a line drawing.

It is said that listening to an instrument being perfectly played or a singer with a beautiful voice can be a magical experience that seeps into your inner being. I believe that looking at quilts can also bring magic to the viewer. It delivers nourishment for the soul through the imagination of the designer in the beauty of the story depicted. With my wish to deliver further magical experiences, I bring you another book on my story quilts.

Yukari Takahara

CONTENTS

Chapter 1 - **Designs**

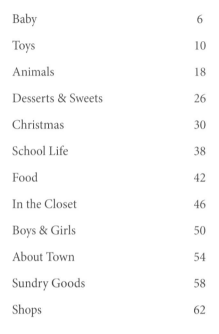

Chapter 2 - **Story Quilts**

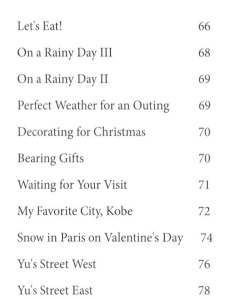

Chapter 3 - **Lessons & Details**

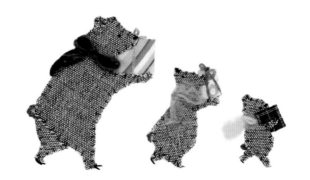

While some of these patterns are useful for smaller quilts, framed or for bags, please feel free to magnify them as large as necessary for your own use.

Baby

Hello! I'm finally here! Look at all the things that Mommy and Daddy bought to welcome me into the world. There's a giraffe, a teddy bear, clothes, and shoes. I'm so happy to be here.

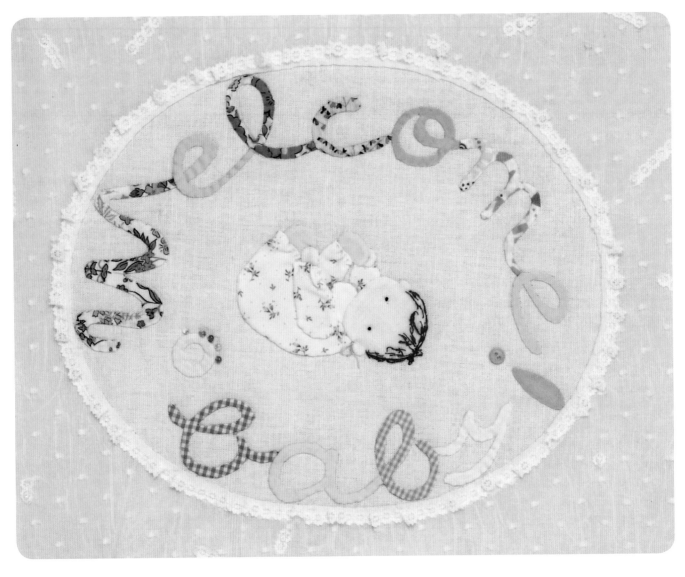

Toys

My shelves are filled with all of my favorite things and friends. See my car and robot and my teddy bear and doll? I love how they have their own special places in my room.

Toys

Animals

Don't you love all kinds of animals? From the birds who chatter outside my window and say hello each day to the bears and reindeer who bring me gifts, I just love all of my animal friends.

Animals

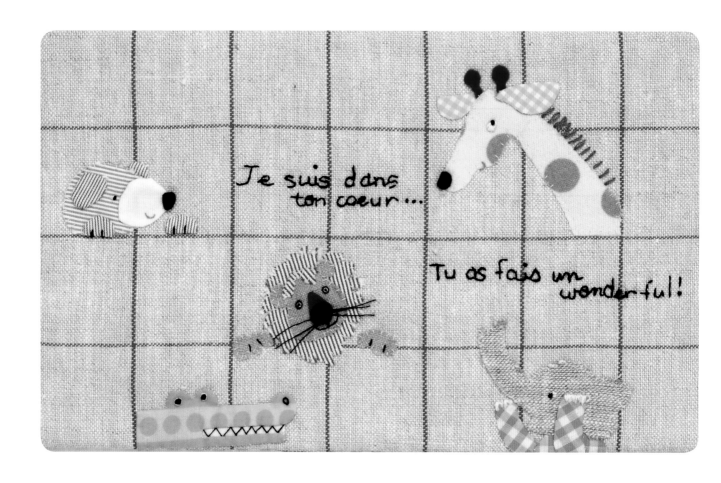

Desserts & Sweets

Sweet and healthy,
er cake is wonderful!

I love to eat all kinds of cakes, cookies, and sweets. Sometimes as a surprise my Dad will bring home a special cake! I am especially lucky as my Mom makes me delicious things to eat all the time.

Christmas

The best thing about the winter beside all the snow is Christmas! I wonder what the North Pole is really like? Don't you wonder how Santa Claus delivers presents to everyone in the city as well as in the country?

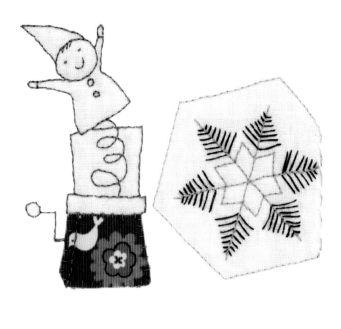

Christmas

School Life

I'm going to be in First Grade this year because I've gotten so big! I'll get to go to the library and get books because I'll learn to read. I love to draw pictures and everyone draws lots of pictures at school. I can't wait to stop and get treats on the way home from school. I'm going to school!

Food

There are a lot of great things about going to school everyday, but the best part is lunchtime! They serve many of my favorite foods, and I always leave with my stomach happy and full.

In the Closet

My mom sews many of my clothes. I love them all so much it is hard to decide which one to wear. OK! I've decided! Let's go out somewhere.

Boys & Girls

Look at all the older girls at the bus stop. They are so fashionable and chic. We love to have trendy clothes, but we grow so fast that it is hard for us to keep up. At least our hats are always cool!

About Town

It's always a thrill to walk around town, wondering what will be new and exciting. When I was little, my Mom brought me, holding my hand. I am old enough now to go alone, but I'd still rather go with my Mom.

flower

Sundry Goods

My mom loves to collect antiques and display them in her cupboards. My favorite collection is one that has all kinds of tea pots and tea cup sets with floral patterns all over them. When I grow up, I want to have a cupboard where I can collect pretty things.

Shops

My absolute favorite shop is the toy store! Looking in the window before going in the shop is almost as much fun as seeing all the wonderful stuffed animals that are inside.

63

Story Quilts

Let's Eat!

On a Rainy Day III

On a Rainy Day II

Perfect Weather for an Outing

Decorating for Christmas

Bearing Gifts

Waiting for Your Visit

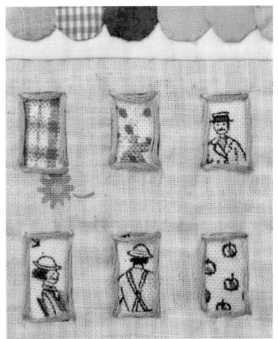

My Favorite City, Kobe

Snow in Paris on Valentine's Day

Little Yu's Street West

"Le Prince"

ANTIQUE

Patisseries à Paris

Basic Appliqué Lessons

The art of appliqué is created by taking one or more small pieces of fabric that depict a part or the whole of a motif, then sewing them to a foundational piece of fabric to create a design. In this basic lesson, I will walk you through the steps I take to create a house or building. We will need the walls, roof, windows, door, and other design elements that you want to make it unique.

Notions & Tools You Will Need to Begin

Tracing paper, heavyweight paper for templates, light table, Chaco paper, or other chalk-based pattern transfer paper, ballpoint pen, pencil, scissors, background fabric (what you will appliqué onto), batting, fabric scraps or fat quarters for your appliqué pieces, embroidery floss, basting thread, quilting/appliqué thread, needles, ribbon, yarn, or other materials for embellishments.

How to Make a Building

Step **1**

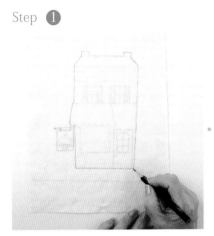

On a flat surface, place the background fabric, which will be the base fabric for your appliqué, right side up on top of the design. Using a pencil, or any other marking tool that you prefer, trace the outlines of the main sections that you will piece or appliqué.

If you cannot see through the fabric, use a light table, or tape the design and fabric in place to a window with bright light. Once the design has been transferred to the background fabric, lay it on top of a piece of batting; baste together.

Step **2**

Make a copy of the original design so that you can cut out the appliqué sections. You might need to make more than one copy. Cut out each section so that you can use these paper pieces as templates. If you don't have a copier, plain paper can also be used; trace each section separately and cut them out.

Place each template on top of the fabric that you have chosen to appliqué for that section of the design and trace around the outside using a marking pencil.

Cut out around the outside lines of the piece being sure to leave a 0.5 cm [¼"] seam allowance. You will not need to add any seam allowance if another section will be appliquéd on top of it. This will help to keep the thickness to a minimum.

Step **3**

Windows and doors often benefit from using the reverse appliqué technique. Reverse appliqué is when you turn the seam allowance within a design area under in order to let the fabric below show through, Use sharp scissors to very carefully cut into the corners at a diagonal just up to the marked line.

Step **4**

Before beginning to stitch the sections down to the background fabric, lay each piece out to make sure all the pieces are prepared and you understand the order in which they should be appliquéd. Always start by appliquéing the pieces in order starting from the bottommost and working your way to the top. Remember that you do not need to appliqué down areas that will be covered by other pieces.

In this case, start with the second story of the building. Pin the piece in place on the background fabric, matching the edges to the marked lines. Stitch down only the sides as the other areas will be covered.

Step **5**

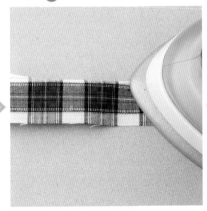

For small pieces that have straight edges, it might be easier to iron the seam allowances under.

Step **6**

Iron three sides of the chimneys under; pin them in place, then appliqué them down leaving the bottom edge open. Iron all four sides of the roof's seam allowance under; pin in place matching the marked lines. Appliqué the roof down, covering the bottoms of the chimneys and the top of the second story.

Step ⑦

Next, appliqué the windows in place (floral fabric), being sure to cover the raw edges of the openings. Follow the windows by appliquéing the shutters on either side of the windows (striped fabric).

Step ⑧

Place the first story in place on the background fabric, covering raw edges, and stitch all the way around the four sides.

Step ⑨

Use an awl or other tool to push the piece of fabric that will be seen through the window into the opening.

Pin the inner window piece in place. Folding the seam allowances under, use the reverse appliqué technique and blindstitch around the window opening.

Step ⑩

Using two strands of embroidery floss and an Outline Stitch, embroider around the inside edges of the window as well as the window sashing.

Step ⑪

Appliqué the door in place (red fabric) around the four sides. Follow the directions in Step 9 above to make the glass window in the door. Outline the glass panes and sashing as in Step 10.
Complete the design by adding the doorknob, mail slot, awning, signage, and the ribbon across the second floor.

Detailed Design Elements

The doorknob is made from a button, while the mail slot is a long bead. The signage with the cake design comes from a label that is appliquéd in place. Embroider the metal rod holding up the signage using the Backstitch. The awning is blindstitched in place along the top and sides, leaving the bottom open to add dimension. Stitch the ribbon in place on the second floor. Finally, feel free to add any other embellishments.

Full-size Pattern

* add 0.5 cm [¼"] seam allowance to the appliqué pieces below.

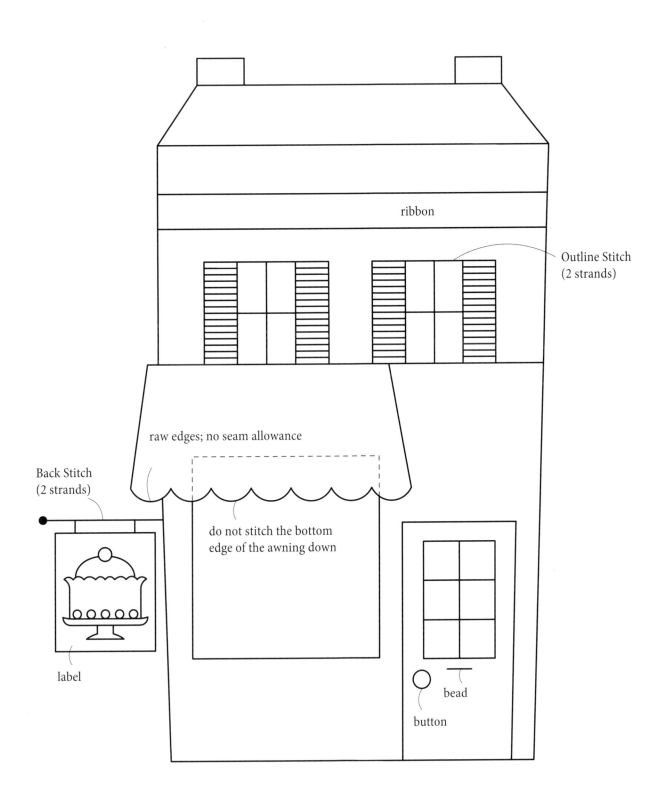

ribbon

Outline Stitch
(2 strands)

raw edges; no seam allowance

Back Stitch
(2 strands)

do not stitch the bottom
edge of the awning down

label

bead

button

Advanced Designs

I find that one of the most fun and satisfying steps of making my quilts is making the detailed decisions within each design. Depending on the fabric, fibers, or embellishments used, the look and feel of a piece can be completely changed.

Making Expressive Faces

(p. 67)

For characters whose faces are facing forward, I always try to add as many facial features as possible. For this little girl, I added expressive eyes and slightly raised eyebrows.

(p. 67)

This little boy is mostly turned away and you only see part of his profile. The focus is put on his hair. To get the appearance of volume in the hair, I use fabric that has thin lines or strips and appliqué it on to imitate the direction of hair. I then use embroidery floss and stitch around the perimeter as strands of hair.

(p. 66)

If the character is facing sideways and you are adding facial features such as eyes, eyebrows, nose or mouth, you want to think about alignment. It often looks best if you align the height of the eyes with the nose.

(p. 66)

This little girl is also a good example of aligning the eyes with the nose. If you have difficulty determining the balance and size of the mouth, you can solve the problem by hiding the mouth with the hand or, in this case, the chopsticks.

(p. 55)

It is always best to start with one or two strands of embroidery floss when adding in any features. This will allow you to get the look you want by taking more stitches if necessary, rather than ripping out. I have also found that showing only the nose in profile can often add a sense of maturity to a character.

(p. 31)

If you want to make a character of a child appear excited or having fun, you can use the simplest of embroidery by adding in the eyes and an open mouth, omitting the nose. Stitch the mouth slightly higher than it would normally be.

Using Other Materials for Embellishments

Ribbon (p. 67)

I have used various patterns and colors of fabric for the different kinds of bread. However, it is also fun to use ribbon embroidery and create three-dimensional objects such as the croissant.

Felt (p. 67)

Felt is a wonderful material to use particularly as the edges won't fray, so you can cut it to the exact sizes you need. I used it for the ham, cheese, and bread for the sandwiches.

Wool (p. 66)

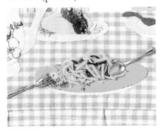

I used yarn to make the spaghetti. Twist and twirl the yarn into a small mound and sew it down. Adding miniature utensils make it absolutely perfect.

Charms (p. 35)

I collect items throughout the year that I think will work well in my quilts. The star, gingerbread man, and reindeer charms are just right to hang up in the little Christmas shop.

Embroidery Floss (p. 59)

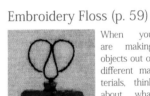

When you are making objects out of different materials, think about what would make it appear the most life-like. To make the ball of yarn, I used embroidery thread and brought it up loosely through the background fabric. Instead of sewing all the strands down, I made them long and criss-crossed them to look like a ball of yarn.

Cording (p. 59)

I used a very fine cording to create the look of a woven basket. Although the lid and handle look the same, I used embroidery floss to create these portions as the stitches are easier to manipulate.

Beads (p. 66)

Beads can be used for many objects. The size and color of these tiny beads were ideal to use for the bunch of grapes. It added a bit of interest to this basket of fruit.

Buttons (p. 66)

I love to use buttons in my quilts. I use them to depict all kinds of things. For this plate of food, I had tiny buttons that became beans in a salad and pickles on top of the hamburgers. Buttons can add the right amount of perspective to flat appliquéd objects.

Buttons (p. 62)

What better way to make a towering pyramid of macaroons for the Patisserie than by using glossy buttons. I used fabric behind them to help make them pop.

Using Embroidery to its best Advantage

Fallen Snow (p. 34)

You can use different types of fiber and floss for embroidery including yarn. I used a white wool yarn to depict snow piled up on top of the roof.

Tree Branches (p. 34)

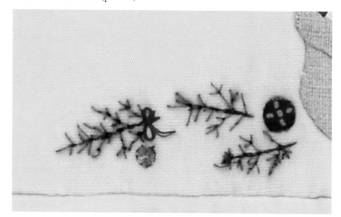

In order to show the fullness of the needles of the fir tree, I used a fine wool mohair. Although it is ultra-fine, it was ideal to give the overall impression of branches.

Windows & Doors (p. 73)

When I have buildings with windows and doors, I think it is fun to have people or objects showing through. If you outline the windows and doors with simple embroidery stitches, such as the Outline Stitch, it will tend to draw the eye.

Glassware & Silverware (p. 67)

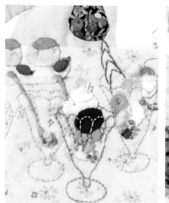

An excellent way to show off glassware or jars is to merely outline them with embroidery stitches. This allows you to see the food, dessert, or beverage inside the glass. I always keep silver, gold, and bronze-colored thread or floss on hand. It is perfect to use when embroidering silverware.

Techniques to use other than Appliqué

Outlining (p. 75)

For a slightly more sophisticated look, you might want to use only one kind of fabric for all the pieces of your appliqué. A great technique that will still allow you to show off the details is to use embroidery floss in a similar color and outline each piece or area.

The quilts I make tend to be quite large and rather epic. Because I do such detailed vignettes, it takes quite a lot of time to do the appliqué and embroidery on this expanse of background fabric. Often I will use mixed media and choose to use a simple pen and ink technique and draw in some areas. If you do this, make sure to use permanent fabric pens.

Pen Drawing (p. 73 top), p. 72 bottom)

You will notice in this vignette of people sitting on a bench, I have drawn the entire thing in pen and ink drawings. I used colored permanent fabric pens to draw in the patterns on the clothes, shoes, hair, etc. Then in order to make it appear to be appliquéd, I simply stitched around most of the drawn objects. This is a really interesting technique for you to try.

Three-Dimensional Objects (p. 42 right)

To add a little texture and fun, I like to put tiny beads inside a bag made of organza. Sew the sides and bottom to the background fabric, slip the beads in, and then secure the top of the bag by tying embroidery floss or thread around the top of the bag.

This technique takes a little planning. Cut the cloth for the basket and baste the part in place that will be inside the basket. Pin the parts of the cloth that will be loose out of the way while you embroider the basket itself. Unpin the rest of the cloth and let it fold down to appear as though it is hanging outside without sewing it. You might choose to fringe the edge of the fabric before you begin.

Printed Fabric (p. 62)

There is a lot of fabric that you can buy that has all kinds of prints on them. I like to collect them in all sizes to have on hand. I find small prints particularly useful to use in windows and doors. It is often difficult to appliqué in areas that are very small, and this is a great way to solve this problem.

Welcome
to our
wedding ceremony

Books
for the
World
of
Tomorrow

Café

Patisseries
à Paris

MICHAEL'S TOY SHOP

Joyeux Noël

welcome baby

ANTIQUE

STORE LOVE

ANTIQUE

Yukari Takahara

Yukari Takahara was born in Kyoto. She graduated from University with a degree in art. In 1992, after teaching in both elementary and middle schools, she and her husband moved back to his hometown. They opened a picture book gallery using their own personal collection. The gallery grew to include a cafe, and a gift and quilt shop called Yuufu-sha. Ms. Takahara teaches crafts and painting from her studio at the same location. In addition to their own art work and activities, they hold many events at Yuufu-sha throughout the year. She is also the author of *Story Quilts - Through the Seasons.*

Yuufu-sha
154-1 Yanochosakaki, Aioi Shi
Hyogo-Ken, Japan 678-0091

http://www.yufusya (Japanese)

Original Title	Story Quilt 2 Tsukihi to Tomoni
Author	Yukari Takahara
	©2012 Yukari Takahara
First Edition	Originally published in Japan in 2012
Published by:	Shufu to Seikatsusha
	3-5-7 Kyoubashi, Chuo-Ku
	Tokyo, Japan 104-8357
	http://www.shufu.co.jp
Translation	©2015 Stitch Publications, LLC
English Translation Rights	arranged with Stitch Publications, LLC through
	Tuttle-Mori Agency, Inc.
Published by:	Stitch Publications, LLC
	P.O. Box 16694
	Seattle, WA 98116
	http://www.stitchpublications.com
Printed & Bound	KHL Printing, Singapore
ISBN	978-0-9863029-0-9
PCN	Library of Congress Control Number: 2014957910

S T o R y Quilt 2

Staff

Book Design	Mami Shiina
Photography	Nobuhiko Honma
Editorial Interview	Keiko Nitta
Illustrations	AD • CHIAKI (Yumika Sakagawa)
Editor	Tomoko Fujii